In the Name of Allah, The All-Merciful,
The Kindest towards believers.

Disclaimer

All rights reserved. No part of this publication may be reproduced, stored in a retrieval system, or transmitted in any form or by any means, electronic, mechanical, photocopying, recording, or otherwise, without the prior written permission of the publisher, except in the case of brief quotations quoted in articles or reviews.

Contact : admin@islamiclessonsmadeeasy.com.au

Visit us :
Facebook.com/islamiclessonsmadeeasy
Youtube.com/islamiclessonsmadeeasy
Instagram.com/islamic_lessons_me
Islamiclessonsmadeeasy.com.au
Ilme.net.au

The pictures used are the property of Islamic Lessons Made Easy. The content and rulings are taken from various leading scholars and are presented in a simplified manner. Therefore, for the exact definition and explanation, please refer to the original sources.

First Edition
©Copyright 2025 Islamic Lessons Made Easy

Contents

Transliteration	4
Introduction	5
Etiquettes of Qurān	6
Sūrah al-Naṣr	8
Summary	20
Glossary	24

Transliteration

ا	a	ق	q
ب	b	ك	k
ت	t	ل	l
ث	th	م	m
ج	j	ن	n
ح	ḥ	ه	h
خ	kh	و	w
د	d	ي	y
ذ	dh	ئ / آ / ـا	ā
ر	r	ـِي	ī
ز	z	ـُو	ū
س	s		
ش	sh		
ص	ṣ		
ض	ḍ		
ط	ṭ		
ظ	ẓ		
ع	ʿ		
غ	gh		
ف	f		

ْ	Read with a sudden pause of air.
ﷺ	Blessings of Allah be upon him and his family.
عليها السلام	Peace be upon her.
عليه السلام	Peace be upon him.
ﷻ	Glorious and Exalted Is He.

Introduction

Tafsīr is an Arabic word that means 'explanation'; it helps us understand what the verses of the Qurān really mean. Scholars study the Qurān by looking at its language, the history behind the verses and other aspects. They also think about how the verses were revealed and how we can use these teachings in our daily lives.

Tafsīr helps us connect with our faith and learn how to use the lessons of the Qurān today. It makes the wisdom of the Qurān easier to understand and more useful for us.

When we made this *Tafsīr*, we worked hard to gather ideas from trusted scholars and important books. We wanted to explain the Qurān in a way that is easy for you to understand.

We hope this *Tafsīr* helps you on your journey to learn more about the Qurān and your faith.

Etiquettes of Qurān

Before reciting, it is recommended to say:

أَعُوذُ بِاللَّهِ مِنَ الشَّيْطَانِ الرَّجِيمِ

Aʿūdhu billāhi minash shayṭānir rajīm

I seek refuge with Allah from the accursed devil.

Then say:

بِسْمِ اللَّهِ الرَّحْمَٰنِ الرَّحِيمِ

Bismillāhir Raḥmānir Raḥīm

In the name of Allah, The Most Gracious, The Most Merciful.

- Make sure you have performed *Wuḍū* before touching any verse of the Qurān
- When reading the Qurān, it is better to face the *Qiblah*
- Make sure that the place where the Qurān is read is free from impurities
- Don't put the Qurān on the ground or anywhere it might get dirty
- Don't place anything on top of the Qurān
- When you recite the Qurān, try to pronounce the words correctly
- Take time to reflect on what the verses mean

After finishing your recitation, say:

صَدَقَ اللَّهُ العَلِيُّ العَظِيمُ

Ṣadaq Allāhul ʿAliyyul ʿAẓīm

Allah, the Sublime, the Great, has spoken the truth.

Sūrah al-Naṣr

Sūrah al-Naṣr

Sūrah al-Naṣr is the 110th chapter of the Qurān.

This chapter was revealed towards the end of the life of Prophet Muhammad ﷺ and is often seen as a prophecy of the victory of Islam.

The chapter teaches us an important lesson: that even when we succeed, we should remember to thank Allah ﷻ and ask for His forgiveness.

When this *Sūrah* was revealed, the Prophet ﷺ shared it with his Companions, and they felt joy and hope for the future. However, his uncle, ʿAbbās, began to cry when he heard it.

The Prophet ﷺ asked him,
"What makes you cry, my uncle?"

ʿAbbās responded,
"I feel this *Sūrah* is a sign of your death, O Messenger of God."

The Prophet ﷺ replied,
"That is indeed as you say."

This interaction shows how this *Sūrah* not only celebrated the victory of Islam but also hinted at the death of the Holy Prophet ﷺ.

The Holy Prophet ﷺ:

The one who recites Sūrah al-Naṣr receives the same reward as if they had been with the Prophet ﷺ during the conquest of Mecca.

(Majmaʿ al-Bayān)

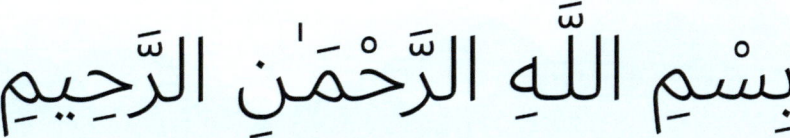

Bismillāhir Raḥmānir Raḥīm

In the Name of Allah, The Most Gracious, The Most Merciful.

إِذَا جَآءَ نَصْرُ ٱللَّهِ وَٱلْفَتْحُ

Idhā jā-a naṣrul lāhi wal fatḥ

When the help and victory comes from Allah.

This verse refers to the time when the Prophet ﷺ and his followers were forced out of Mecca and faced years of hardship and exile.

After going through so many hardships, Allah ﷻ assures them that victory is near, and they will soon return to Mecca successfully.

It was a message of hope, reassuring the Prophet ﷺ and his companions that their efforts were not wasted and that divine help was coming soon to bring them success.

وَرَأَيْتَ ٱلنَّاسَ يَدْخُلُونَ فِي دِينِ ٱللَّهِ أَفْوَاجًا

Wara-aytan nāsa yadkhulūna fī dīnil lāhi afwājā

And when you see the people entering the Religion of Allah in large crowds.

This verse refers to when the Prophet ﷺ and his followers returned to Mecca victorious after years of hardship. They witnessed large groups of people embracing Islam willingly, without the need for battle.

The conquest of Mecca was one of Islam's greatest victories—not only because it happened without bloodshed but also because it proved to many Arabs that the Prophet ﷺ was indeed truthful. They believed that if he had been a false messenger, Allah ﷻ would not have allowed him to conquer Mecca. This victory strengthened their belief in the Prophet ﷺ.

فَسَبِّحْ بِحَمْدِ رَبِّكَ وَاسْتَغْفِرْهُ ۚ إِنَّهُ كَانَ تَوَّابًا

Fasabbiḥ biḥamdi rabbika wastaghfirh, innahū kāna tawwābā

Then glorify and praise your Lord and seek His forgiveness. Indeed, He is the one who accepts repentance.

So, Allah ﷻ is saying that when He grants you victory and you witness crowds of people entering Islam freely, instead of displaying pride or seeking revenge for what the people of Mecca did, He provides three crucial instructions:

Sabbiḥ (سَبِّحْ): This means to acknowledge and glorify Allah ﷻ as completely pure and free from any imperfection.

Ḥamd (حَمد): Then, we praise and thank Allah ﷻ. This is a way to express our gratitude for His blessings and mercy.

Istighfār (اسْتِغْفَار): Then, we seek forgiveness from Allah ﷻ. While Allah ﷻ is perfect and free of flaws, we are weak, ignorant and sometimes unjust. *Istighfār* acknowledges our imperfections before Allah ﷻ.

This *Sūrah* reveals that the help of Allah ﷻ comes first, followed by victory. It declares that when the victory of Allah ﷻ arrives, many people will choose to enter Islam in large numbers. After this victory, the Holy Prophet ﷺ is instructed to praise Allah ﷻ and seek His forgiveness.

It's important to note that when the Prophet ﷺ does *istighfār* (seeks forgiveness), it does not imply he has sinned. Instead, he seeks help and protection from Allah ﷻ for himself and his followers against the forces of evil and asks for forgiveness on their behalf.

From this *Sūrah*, we learn that victory comes from Allah ﷻ through our struggles. We must be patient, as some challenges may last for years. It is essential to remember that Allah ﷻ can guide us out of any difficulty, so we should always turn to Him and express our gratitude.

We should not view our acts of worship as reasons for pride or arrogance. While they may lead to success, we must recognise that we could not have accomplished them without the blessings and support of Allah ﷻ.

When we acknowledge the victories and blessings from Allah ﷻ, we should sincerely thank Him and seek forgiveness for our shortcomings.

Glossary

Ḥamd	- Praise
Istighfār	- Seek forgiveness
Naṣr	- Help, Victory
Qiblah	- Direction of the Ka'bah
Sabbiḥ	- Glorify
Sūrah	- Chapter
Sūrah al-Naṣr	- Chapter of Divine Help

Credit

All praise belongs to Allah, the All Merciful towards all existents, the Kindest towards believers. He Who has given us enough patience and courage to complete this book.

Islamic Lessons Made Easy would like to thank all those involved in this project for their hard work and commitment.

CREATOR	EDITORS
Abbas Ibrahim	Kawthar Ibrahim
	Sheikh Dr Zaid Alsalami

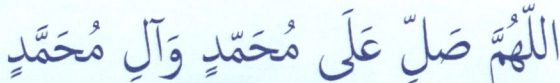

Allahumma ṣalli ʿala Muḥammadi(n)w wa āli Muḥammad
O Allah, (please do) bless Muḥammad and the Household of Muḥammad

Contact: admin@islamiclessonsmadeeasy.com.au

Visit us:
Facebook.com/islamiclessonsmadeeasy
Youtube.com/islamiclessonsmadeeasy
Instagram.com/islamic_lessons_me
Islamiclessonsmadeeasy.com.au
Ilme.net.au

www.ingramcontent.com/pod-product-compliance
Lightning Source LLC
Chambersburg PA
CBRC091203070526
44583CB00008B/185